CRAIG KIELBURGER

LESSONS FROM a STREET KID

ILLUSTRATED BY
MARISA ANTONELLO
& VICTORIA LAIDLEY

Hi! My name is Craig Kielburger.

When I was 12, I was looking for the comics in my newspaper and saw a story on the front page about a young boy in Pakistan.

When he was 4-years-old he started working in a carpet factory. He escaped when he was 10-years-old to tell others about what happened to him. When he was 12, he was killed because he was talking out against child labour. I was really upset. He was the same age as me! I tore the story out of the paper and took it to school with me. I showed it to my class and 11 of my classmates wanted to join me. We started as a group of 12 students, all 12-years-old. We called our club Free The Children. We would hold fundraisers and raise money to send to countries like India, Kenya, Haiti and Brazil.

We were just kids helping other kids!

Over the years, Free The Children grew as more young people joined us. I started travelling while in elementary school to meet some of these children that we were helping. I travelled to Brazil to meet some of the thousands of children that live on the streets. These are children without a home or family, and they can't go to school.

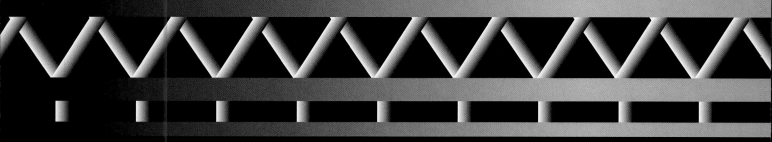

This is the true story of my first trip to Brazil, and the lessons I learned from my friends there...

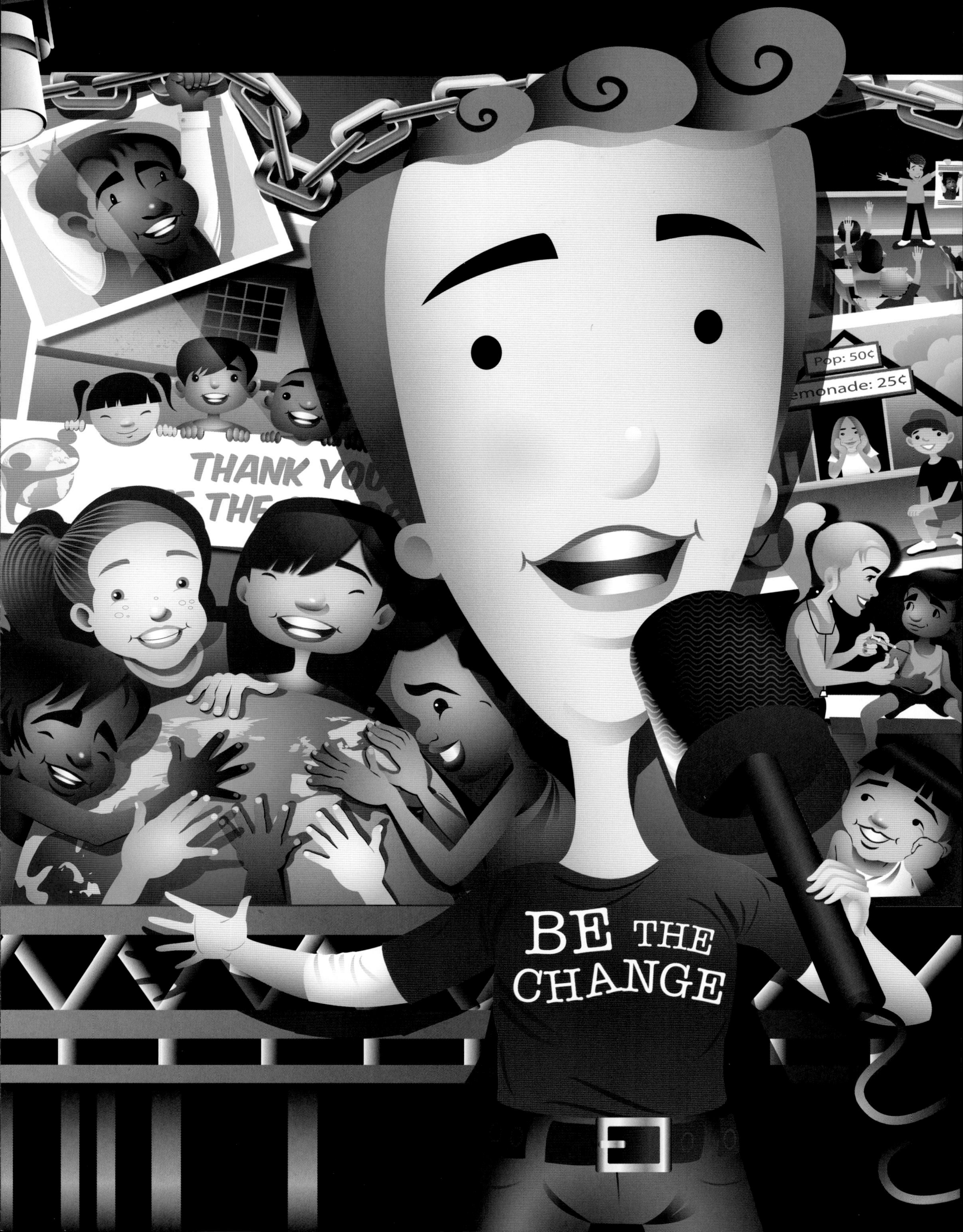
THANK YO
Pop: 50¢
emonade: 25¢
BE THE CHANGE

The smell of Brazil hits me first. It is sweet and fresh like the sea.
Being on the coast, in the city of Salvador, you can smell fish and spices everywhere you go. Brazil is beautiful. Right on the Atlantic Ocean in South America the ocean breeze is fresh. It takes me a little while to figure out the language that everyone is speaking. A street vendor tells me it is Portuguese.

Café
Take A Load Off

Specials:
Coffee: $2.45
Big Coffee: $3.50
Even Bigger Coffee: $7.00

Standing in the street, the sun is hot on our backs as people move in all directions around me. Dogs run free in the streets searching for food. Birds circle above and seagulls squawk by the ocean's edge. Tourists enjoy cups of coffee sitting in small shops. There are lots of big beaches and fancy carnivals—lots of people are dressed in bright costumes!

But it's the children that I *see* first.

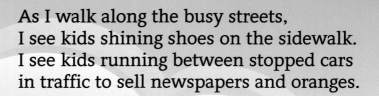

As I walk along the busy streets,
I see kids shining shoes on the sidewalk.
I see kids running between stopped cars
in traffic to sell newspapers and oranges.

I see a couple of kids doing acrobats
and begging for money from tourists.
"Get your daily newspaper. Get it here,"
one young boy yells.

I can't believe my eyes as kids my own age are working in the streets!

I walk up to a young boy with dark hair and a ripped green shirt. He's shining an older person's shoes on the sidewalk beside me.
"Hey there, what's your name?" I ask him, kneeling down beside him.
"My name is Alberto. Can I shine your shoes next?"

I look down at my shoes. I'm wearing running shoes.
"Oh no, it's OK," I say. "Thank you, but I would—"

All of a sudden I hear the screech
of car brakes behind me.

SCREECH!

A young boy with a red and black soccer jersey is being helped off the street by his friend. A driver in a blue pick-up truck is yelling at the boy for getting in his way.

"Are you OK?" I ask, worried. "What just happened?"
"Yes, I am fine. I was just trying to sell oranges and the driver almost hit me," he says. He looks at me. "Do you want to buy an orange?"

I see his small body and his dirty, ripped jeans. He has smudged dirt on his face and no shoes.

"I have a better idea. Can I buy you lunch?" I ask.
"My name is Craig."
"Lunch? You're buying? Yes!" he says, jumping in the air.

"So what's your name?" I ask as we walk to the market.
 "My name is José. Can I have a hot dog? Actually, can I have two…
no, three hot dogs?"
 "Yes, you can have three hot dogs," I laugh.

We sit on the sidewalk and I ask José where he lives.
 "Here," he points all around him. "I don't have a house. I live with my
friends in a bus shelter. You should come see it. We're a big family."

As we walk through Salvador's streets, José tells me why he left his home. After his father left to find work, his mother couldn't afford to take care of José and his five siblings.

"We were really poor. My Mom needed help bringing money home. That's when I left. I haven't been back," José says, looking down at the street as he talks. "I miss them, but I have another family now. My friends and I take care of each other on the streets. If someone in our family of street kids gets sick, we all help them. We will put our money together to get them some medicine. I also do my best to play doctor," José laughs.

All their faces are dirty, but their smiles are big. In a large group, the street kids all run up to me and grab my hands. They laugh as they point to my blonde hair. José still has two hot dogs and gives them to the other kids to share. They each take a bite and pass the hot dogs around.

Their house is a broken down bus stop. They have cardboard spread out on the floor. They use newspapers as blankets to stay warm at night. One of the children I saw earlier doing acrobats in the street runs up to me.
"Are you with the business owners?" he asks me.

"No, I'm just a friend of José's," I say, surprised at his question. "Why?"

"Because the business owners don't want us to sleep in front of their stores. They will pour cold water on us when we are sleeping," says the young boy, still wearing the same dirty shirt as before. "Sometimes they will pick us up and drop us outside of the city."

Behind us a group of the kids burst into song.
Before the boy can tell me more,
José and his friends are pulling me
to join in the dance.

We dance and sing at the top of our lungs. We use old cans and barrels as drums. One of the boys has an old horn that he blows making a squawk sound. Some use broken brooms as make-believe guitars.

And everyone else just claps their hands and stomps their feet as we dance in a circle.

José asks if I want to play soccer.
I look around but don't see a ball to
play with. José watches me look around
and grabs an empty water bottle on the
ground. "Here we go. We'll use this!" he
says with a big smile. "Let's go play!"

After scoring a goal, the goalie falls on the water bottle and crushes it. Everyone laughs and pats each other on the back for a good game.

"Don't you usually play with a soccer ball?" I ask, trying to catch my breath.
"We have never played with a real ball. None of us can afford to buy one," says José with a shrug.
"We play ice hockey in Canada where I am from," I say. José just laughs as I try to explain the game because he has never seen snow before.
"I rather play soccer," says José with a laugh. "That sounds too cold for me!"

As it gets late, I say goodbye to my new friends.
"Thank you for showing me your home today," I say to José. "And for the soccer game."

As I am about to leave, José calls after me to stop. "Thank you for coming to see my family," he says with a smile. "I want to give you something to remember me and my family. I want to give you a gift."

But José doesn't have a home, food or any toys. He doesn't even have a soccer ball to play with.

"It's OK, José, I don't need a gift. Meeting you was a gift itself," I say.
He begins to take off his red and black soccer jersey that he was wearing all day.
"This is for you." he says, handing me the jersey.
"José, I can't take this!" I say. I'm afraid that he will be cold at night. But José doesn't move. His eyes look straight at me. He wants me to have his most prized item, the shirt off his back. He pushes the jersey towards me again.

"If I take this jersey, you need to take my shirt," I say. José nods his head. I take off my simple blue shirt and hand it to him. We trade our T-shirts and put them on.

Looking at me in his jersey, José says: "Now you will be a better soccer player!"

We laugh again as I begin to head back.

José's red and black soccer jersey still hangs in my office at Free The Children. I look at it every day. It always reminds me of the energy and excitement of Brazil.

It reminds me of when I first met José's family of street kids. It reminds me how they took care of each other. It reminds me of our dance party. It reminds me of the soccer match with the water bottle. And it will forever remind me of the lesson of generosity that José taught me. Every day I try to follow his example of giving in all my actions.

And I know that with his generosity, we can all end poverty one day.

ME TO WE TRIPS

Come join me in Kenya on a Me to We Trip. If you want to really experience another culture and truly see the world, take a Me to We Trip. Seek out a volunteer travel experience as a family and see the beautiful Maasailand. Our staff live and work in the communities you'll visit, coordinating schoolbuilding and supporting development in participation with local communities. On a Me to We Trip, you'll learn leadership skills, experience new cultures and forge truly meaningful connections. Over 3,000 adventurous people of all ages have chosen to volunteer abroad with us. You'll do incredible things, like building schools and assisting on clean water projects. You'll meet exuberant children excited at new possibilities for learning, and be immersed in local communities in ways never otherwise possible. And best of all, you'll have memories that last a lifetime.

Visit www.metowe.com/trips to learn more.

ME TO WE SPEAKERS

Bring me as a speaker to your school—and take away all you need to "be the change." The team at Me to We Speakers has traveled the world to discover the most inspirational people with remarkable stories and life experiences. From community activists to former child soldiers to social entrepreneurs, our roster of energetic, experienced speakers are leading the me to we movement: living and working in developing communities, helping businesses achieve social responsibility and inspiring auditoriums of youth and educators to action. Our stories and powerful messages inspire, motivate and educate. We leave audiences with a desire to take action and make a difference. We will make you laugh, cry and gain new perspective on what really matters. Be warned: our passion is contagious!

Visit www.metowe.com/speakers to learn more.

BUY A BOOK, GIVE A BOOK

The Buy a Book, Give a Book promise
ensures that for every Me to We book purchased,
a notebook will be given
to a child in a developing country.

ME TO WE BOOKS

My Maasai Life: A Child's Adventure in Africa
Robin Wiszowaty; Illustrated by Marisa Antonello and Victoria Laidley

Follow a young Robin Wiszowaty as she travels to Kenya for the first time. Living with the Maasai people, Robin explores the land with her new family. Getting water, finding wood and singing songs. And don't forget the zebras, cows and giraffes. It is all a part of the adventure with the Maasai. With Robin as a guide, the full-colour illustrations only enhance any child's own adventure into the world of the Maasai.

It Takes a Child
Craig Kielburger and Marisa Antonello; Illustrated by Turnstyle Imaging

It was an ordinary morning like any other. Twelve-year-old Craig Kielburger woke to his alarm clock and hurried downstairs to wolf down a bowl of cereal over the newspaper's comics before school. But what he discovered on the paper's front page would change his life—and eventually affect over a million young people worldwide. It Takes a Child is a fun, vibrant look back at Craig's adventures throughout South Asia, learning about global poverty and child labour. This incredible story truly demonstrates you're never too young to change the world.

The World Needs Your Kid: Raising Children Who Care and Contribute
Craig Kielburger and Marc Kielburger and Shelley Page

This unique guide to parenting is centred on a simple but profound philosophy that will encourage children to become global citizens. Drawing on life lessons from such remarkable individuals as Jane Goodall, Mia Farrow and Archbishop Desmond Tutu, award-winning journalist Shelley Page and Marc and Craig Kielburger demonstrate how small actions make huge differences in the life of a child and can ultimately change the world.

Free the Children
Craig Kielburger

This is the story that launched a movement. Free the Children recounts twelve-year-old Craig Kielburger's remarkable odyssey across South Asia, meeting some of the world's most disadvantaged children, exploring slums and sweatshops, fighting to rescue children from the chains of inhumane conditions. Winner of the prestigious Christopher Award, Free the Children has been translated into eight languages and inspired young people around the world.

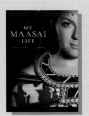

My Maasai Life: From Suburbia to Savannah
Robin Wiszowaty

In her early 20s, Robin Wiszowaty left the ordinary world behind to join a traditional Maasai family. In the sweeping vistas and dusty footpaths of rural Kenya, she embraced a way of life unlike she'd ever known. With full-color photographs from her adventures, Robin's heart-wrenching story will inspire you to question your own definitions of home, happiness and family.

The Making of an Activist
Craig and Marc Kielburger with Lekha Singh

Warning: this book will change you. Full of vivid images and inspiring words, travelogues, poems and sparkling artwork, The Making of an Activist is more than just a scrapbook of Free The Children's remarkable evolution. It's a testament to living an engaged, active and compassionate life, painting an intimate portrait of powerful young activists. Explore the book. Catch the spark.

Visit www.metowe.com/books to learn more.

Craig with José's jersey more than 10 years after the soccer game.